Dog Rock..

Written by June Crebbin
Illustrated by Shahab Shamshirsaz

Collins

Dog runs to a pot to sip.

2

Can Dog get it? No!

Can Cat get it?

No! Cat is in the pot!

Dog tugs Cat. Pop!

Dog sits.

Dog picks up a rock.

Dog tips rocks in the pot.

Dog can get it!

Dog sips.

Cat sips.

Top dog!

Top dog

Ideas for reading

Written by Clare Dowdall, PhD
Lecturer and Primary Literacy Consultant

Learning objectives: *(reading objectives correspond with Pink B band; all other objectives correspond with White band)* read simple words by sounding out and blending the phonemes all through the word from left to right; recognise common digraphs; read a range of familiar and common words and simple sentences independently; draw together ideas and information from across a whole text; give some reasons why things happen or characters change

Curriculum links: Citizenship

Focus phonemes: d, o, g, r, u, n, s, a, p, t, i, c, e, ck

Fast words: the, to, no

Resources: magnetic letters, flashcards of focus phonemes, bowl, small stones or marbles, paper, pens

Word count: 49

Getting started

- Revisit the focus phonemes *d, g, o, ck, e, u, r* using flashcards. Remind children that the *ck* digraph makes one sound.

- Explain that this is a retelling of an Aesop's fable, and explain that these are famous stories that teach us something.

- Read the title together. Practise blending the sounds in the word *r-o-ck-s*. Look at the picture on the front cover. Discuss what *Dog Rocks!* might mean.

- Turn to the blurb. Model how to read it with appropriate expression, noticing the question mark. Ask children to read the blurb with you and check they understand what it refers to.

Reading and responding

- Turn to p2. Model how to read the text, sounding out and blending new words, e.g. *s-i-p*, and then rereading the whole sentence for fluency. Ask children what the word sip means.

- Ask children to read the text on p3. Discuss what problem the dog has.

- Ask children to read to p13 independently. Remind them to blend sounds to read new words, and to reread whole sentences to develop fluency. Use questions to support children to make meaning as they decode.